john

A DOUBLE-EDGED BIBLE STUDY

john

A DOUBLE-EDGED BIBLE STUDY

TH1NK: **Life**Change™ NAVPRESS

NAVPRESS⊘

NavPress is the publishing ministry of The Navigators, an international Christian organization and leader in personal spiritual development. NavPress is committed to helping people grow spiritually and enjoy lives of meaning and hope through personal and group resources that are biblically rooted, culturally relevant, and highly practical.

For a free catalog go to www.NavPress.com
or call 1.800.366.7788 in the United States or 1.800.839.4769 in Canada.

contents

introduction to TH1NK: LifeChange

Double-Edged and Ready for Action

For the word of God is living and active. Sharper than any double-edged sword, it penetrates even to dividing soul and spirit, joints and marrow; it judges the thoughts and attitudes of the heart.

Hebrews 4:12

a reason to study

Studying the Bible is more than homework. It is more than reading a textbook. And it is more than an opportunity for a social gathering. Like Hebrews suggests, the Bible knows us, challenges us, and, yes, judges us. Like a double-edged sword, it's sharp enough to cut through our layers of insecurity and pretense to change our lives forever.

Deep down, isn't that what we want – to actually *experience* God's power in our lives through Scripture? That's what TH1NK: LifeChange is all about. The purpose of this Bible study is to connect you intimately with God's Word. It can change you, not only intellectually but also spiritually, emotionally, maybe even physically. God's Word is that powerful.

The psalmist wrote,

> *What you say goes, GOD,*
> *and stays, as permanent as the heavens.*
> *Your truth never goes out of fashion;*
> *it's as up-to-date as the earth when the sun comes*
> *up. . . .*
> *If your revelation hadn't delighted me so,*
> *I would have given up when the hard times came.*
> *But I'll never forget the advice you gave me;*
> *you saved my life with those wise words.*
> *Save me! I'm all yours.*
> *I look high and low for your words of wisdom.*
> *The wicked lie in ambush to destroy me,*
> *but I'm only concerned with your plans for me.*
> *I see the limits to everything human,*
> *but the horizons can't contain your commands!*
>
> (PSALM 119:89-90,92-96, MSG)

Do you notice the intimate connection the psalmist has with God *because* of the greatness of the Word? He trusts God, he loves Him, and his greatest desire is to obey Him. But the only way he knows how to do any of this is because he knows God's voice, God's words.

the details

Each TH1NK: LifeChange study covers one book of the Bible so you can concentrate on its particular, essential details. Although every study covers a different book, there are common threads throughout the series. Each study will do the following:

1. Help you understand the book you're studying so well that it affects your daily thinking
2. Teach valuable Bible study skills you can use on your own to go even deeper into God's Word
3. Provide a contextual understanding of the book, offering historical background, word definitions, and explanatory notes
4. Allow you to understand the message of the book as a whole
5. Demonstrate how God's Word can transform you into a bona fide representative of Jesus

Every week, plan on spending about thirty to forty-five minutes on your own to complete the study. Then get together with your group. Depending on the amount of time it takes, you can either go through a whole or a half lesson each week. If you do one lesson per week, you'll finish the study in just under three months. But it's all up to you.

the structure

The thirteen lessons include the following elements:

Study. First you'll study the book by yourself. This is where you'll answer questions, learn cultural and biographical information, and ask God some questions of your own.

Live. After you've absorbed the information, you'll want to look in a mirror – figuratively, that is. Think about your life in the context of what you've learned. This is a time to be honest with yourself and with God about who you are and how you are living.

Connect. You know that a small-group study time isn't just for hanging out and drinking soda. A small group provides accountability and support. It's one thing to say to yourself, *I'm really going to work on this* and entirely another thing to say it to a group of your friends. Your friends can support your decisions, encourage you to follow through, and pray for you regularly. And vice versa.

In your group, you'll want to talk with each other about what you discovered on your own, things that went unanswered, things that challenged you, and things that changed you. Use the guidance in this section to lead your discussion. After that, pray for each other.

Go deeper. Thirsty for more? Just can't get enough? Then use the guidance in this section to explore even deeper the vastness of Scripture. It's similar to extra credit for all you overachievers who love to learn.

Memory verse of the week. Did a particular verse make you think? Is there a verse you can't get out of your head? Write it down and memorize it. Allow God's Word to permanently brand itself in your head and your heart.

Notes from group discussion. At the end of each chapter, there are some pages for notes. Use them to ask questions of God or yourself, to write important verses and observations, or for anything else you want to jot down.

now go!

You are now ready to experience God and the Bible in an intense new way. So jump in headfirst. Allow the double-edged sword of Scripture to pierce your mind, your heart, your life.

the beloved story

Take a look at this page. Not at the words on it, but at the page itself. Pretty easy to understand, right? Made of paper, bound on one side, cut crisp and straight on three other sides. Two corners made of perfect right angles. No big deal.

Pages are easy to understand on their fundamental level as part of a book. But dig a little deeper, and what will you find? Intersecting fibers of wood, marvelously compressed to be rigid, yet foldable. Dig deeper and you'll find an intricate, mind-blowing, molecular dance of protons, neutrons, and electrons, something so complex and minute it cannot even be photographed.

The gospel of John is, in many ways, just like the page you're reading. On one hand, it is a fascinating read for those who want a first introduction to Jesus. It's simple enough to follow and clear enough in its language for anyone to "get it" the first time. But on the other hand, it is complex and deep, a book that could merit years of study. It welcomes the humble while challenging the wise. In other words, the gospel itself is like the Man about whom it was written.

who wrote it?

Tradition holds that this gospel was written by the apostle John, and while that tradition has recently come up for debate,[1] we do know that it was written by a Jew from Palestine who either personally saw or had access to eyewitness testimony of Jesus' life. We also know that the author had a lot of authority in the newly founded church and that the gospel was written before AD 100, probably around the end of John's life.

the point?

God uniquely inspired four different men to write four different accounts of Jesus' life – four gospel accounts that would bear God's authority. The first three, gospels Matthew, Mark, and Luke (collectively known as the Synoptic Gospels), focus on Jesus' ministry in Galilee, as well as His last week in Jerusalem. John, on the other hand, spends most of his time on Jesus in Jerusalem, focusing instead on His identity and mission.

Many Jews believed the Messiah, whenever He came, would be a political king who would overthrow the Roman government and reestablish Israel; when Jesus showed up and did neither of these things, these Jews became confused about Jesus and His mission. John seemed to have written his gospel as a means of explaining to the Jews exactly who Jesus was and how He was the Messiah. Also, because the gospel of John often explains Jewish customs, it appears as if John wanted to make sure Gentile believers fully understood Jesus' mission.

preconceived notions

The Word became flesh and
made his dwelling among us.
We have seen his glory, the
glory of the One and Only, who
came from the Father, full of
grace and truth.

John 1:14

It's happened to all of us. You're expecting a phone call from a familiar person, maybe your mom, or a friend. The phone rings and, thinking you're going to have a laugh or two, you answer it in a casual or funny way. But your laughter quickly turns to embarrassment as you realize that, instead of a familiar voice, you're talking to your church's head pastor. Things don't always work out like we expect them to.

Now think of Jesus coming on the scene in ancient Israel, where people had been expecting a Messiah to show up on their doorstep. They had all sorts of ideas of what the Messiah would look like, and Jesus didn't really match up with those ideas. At all.

But there was something about Him that made them think. Why did He come there? Was He really the Messiah, the one who was supposed to restore Israel? If He was, why didn't He look like it? These are the questions that plagued people as Jesus walked the earth. Many of them just didn't understand Him; He completely defied their preconceived notions of what the Messiah looked like.

It is with this mindset that John wrote his gospel, so that people could get a clear picture of Jesus – and a true understanding of the Messiah who really was knocking on their door, hoping to come in.

1 It'd be hard to study John without first knowing what's contained in the book, so take some time right now to read it straight through, as you would a novel or a feature magazine article. Don't get caught up in the details; that's for later. Once you finish, gather your thoughts in these areas:

Your first impressions

Repeated words or phrases

General themes

What you learned about Jesus

Your favorite part

What you felt after you finished it

John's main purpose in writing it

live

2 Look over what you've written so far. Pray. What does God want you to get out of this study? What specific areas of your life need to change and grow?

3 What can you do in the next week to help in these areas?

connect

In your group, talk about your individual first impressions of what you've read in John. Share your ideas with each other, encouraging a sense of common purpose. Discuss your goals as a group, as well as your individual goals. Pray together for support and wisdom as you journey through the gospel of John as a group.

go deeper

What was one of the key ideas you found in John – something that resonated with you the most? Seek out other passages in the Bible that focus on the idea, and write down the correlations with the gospel of John.

memory verse of the week

Did a particular verse make you think? Is there a verse you can't get out of your head? Write it down and memorize it. Allow God's Word to permanently brand itself in your head and your heart.

notes from group discussion

the meanings of words

In the beginning was the Word, and the Word was with God, and the Word was God. He was with God in the beginning.

John 1:1-2

First impressions. Aren't they tough? Trying to make a good first impression, especially when you know you're going to be different from other people who are *also* trying to make a good first impression, can be a harrowing experience.

In writing his gospel, John definitely stands out on the "first impression" front. Matthew and Luke start off with Jesus' birth, Mark with His baptism. It's interesting, then, how John starts from the very beginning and then moves directly into Jesus' arrival in the desert for His baptism.

Interspersed is the testimony of John the Baptist, the first legitimate prophet to appear in Israel in four hundred years. Known throughout the region, John the Baptist was adored by the crowds, grudgingly respected by religious leaders, and feared by the authorities.

Read the first chapter of John.

1 Repetition is a major feature of John's style. What words does he repeat in this first chapter? Keep this repetition in mind as you continue to read through this book in the coming days and weeks.

2 What does John say about the Word? Who or what is the Word? What does He do?

Word (1:1). John uses the word *Logos* here to describe "the Word," a term which the Jews used to describe how God created the universe, guided the prophets, delivered His people, and accomplished His will. Gentile readers understood it as the eternal, impersonal, deity-like Reason (or Intelligence) that pervaded and directed everything in the universe. Either way, *Logos* carried a lot of powerful theological implications.

fyi

3 What was the Father's role in creation?

The Son's?

fyi

• *Made his dwelling among us (1:14).* In the original Greek, this means "to pitch one's tent." To the knowledgeable Jew, John is clearly drawing parallels between Jesus' arrival on earth and the glory of God once seen in the traveling tabernacle of the Old Testament. The Word is no longer seen as a fiery cloud; now the Word is fully human.

• Have a question about something you just read? Write it down as soon as you think of it. Review it later to see if the Holy Spirit might be using it to prompt you in a certain direction.

4 What did John the Baptist testify about Jesus in 1:29-34?

5 How would you put this in your own words?

• *Pharisees (1:24).* This name means "separated ones," as the Pharisees separated themselves by focusing on strictly following the Law of Moses, down to the letter. Where the Sadducees were considered the party of the aristocrats and chief priests, the Pharisees were more interested in the common people and were the real moral authority of the Jews. Many Pharisees saw themselves as experts on God's system, so when John the Baptist showed up preaching and baptizing, they just had to know what he was really up to.

• *Son of Man (1:51).* Jesus often referred to Himself this way, and it most likely came from Ezekiel 4:1–5:17, where God called the prophet Ezekiel "son of man" and then commanded him to bear Israel's sin symbolically. The odds are good that Jesus used this term because it didn't have political implications, like *Messiah* did.

6 In 1:51, Jesus is obviously making a parallel between Himself and Jacob's dream in Genesis 28:10-12. Why is He comparing Himself to a staircase between heaven and earth?

live

7a Reading through 1:1-18, think about how this passage affects you personally. How does it affect you that Jesus is the Word? What about that He is God? That God used Him to create all things? That He became flesh and dwelt among us?

7b Look through your answers. What can you *specifically* do to have these things affect your character?

8 How are you, like John the Baptist, called to prepare others for the Lord's coming? How are you carrying this out? How can you improve?

connect

In your group, discuss the power of words. What are some things in this passage you each individually would like to act on? What about as a group? What have you learned about yourselves since your group last met?

Jews used terms such as "light," "living water," and "bread" to describe the Law of God, symbols Jesus also used. Why did He do that? Focus on whichever one of these attributes speaks to you the most, and spend five minutes each day this week thanking Jesus for being who He is.

memory verse of the week

Did a particular verse make you think? Is there a verse you can't get out of your head? Write it down and memorize it. Allow God's Word to permanently brand itself in your head and your heart.

notes from group discussion

the beginning of miracles

Lesson 3

This, the first of his miraculous signs, Jesus performed at Cana in Galilee. He thus revealed his glory, and his disciples put their faith in him.

John 2:11

Superhero movies are all the rage these days, and part of the reason, outside of the nonstop action and crazy CG effects, is that viewers particularly like to see how these heroes first discover and use their superpowers. In the superhero industry, this is called the "origin story." We like to experience with our heroes their first steps with their newfound powers and see how they put those powers to work for the good of mankind.

Jesus is far from a superhero – much better in fact – but He does have His own "origin story." He's only five days into His public ministry and He's begun to gather some disciples. Now He's gone to Galilee, ready to start His ministry there. What will be the first of His many acts? How will He kick off His ministry? How will He introduce Himself to people? The origin story has begun.

Read the second chapter of John.

fyi

• *Wedding (2:1)*. The bride and groom would take a torch-
lit procession to the groom's house, where they would
then host a celebratory wedding feast that often lasted as long as
a week.[1] In the Old Testament, weddings symbolized the eventual
coming of the Messiah, when God would again "marry" Israel, His
beloved bride.

• *No more wine (2:3)*. The wedding feast was a very serious issue,
and hospitality failure was seen as a major blot on the family's repu-
tation. In fact, if guests were so inclined, they could take legal action
against a host who'd failed them. When the wine ran out, there was
more at stake than just social embarrassment—the groom and his
family could have received a stout fine.[2]

• *Six stone water jars (2:6)*. Daily life in a secular world frequently
made the Jews ceremonially unclean, so they kept a lot of water
around to pour over their hands before they ate or studied the law.
This particular household, full of guests, had a total capacity of over
120 gallons.

1 How did Jesus' first miraculous act affect His disciples (2:11)?

2 How did it reveal Jesus' character? His identity? His mission?

3   Why did Jesus choose this act as His first miracle? Make a list of as many reasons as you can think of.

fyi   *Temple (2:14).* This temple, halfway under construction at the time, was surrounded by courts, but the outer court was the only one accessible to Gentiles, and it was from here, most likely, that Jesus drove out the merchants. While their trade was necessary (people who'd traveled hundreds of miles likely couldn't have brought sacrificial animals with them, and foreign coins had to be exchanged for proper currency), it shouldn't have been taking place inside the temple, where the noise and disruption would have made it impossible for Gentiles to meet with and worship God.[3]

4   Why did Jesus feel so strongly about the merchants and loan sharks in the temple (2:13-17)?

5   How did this incident reveal Jesus' character? His identity? His mission?

6   Why did Jesus have the authority to toss out the merchants and loan sharks (2:18-22)?

> live

7   Why did Jesus choose to turn the Jewish water of purification into wine? How is this act of changing dirty water into wedding wine significant for you?

8   What insight from John chapter 2 is most important to you?

9   How can you let this affect your life?

connect

Here's a tricky question for your group: Is Jesus more interested in love and joy than in justice and holiness? Consider the responses in light of the two actions Jesus performed in this week's reading. Then pray together, thanking Jesus for being the one who transforms water into wine, human religion into a relationship with God. Praise Him for insisting on the purity of His Father's house of worship, and thank Him for becoming the true temple that replaced the man-made one.

go deeper

Take a look at Matthew 21:12-13, Mark 11:15-17, and Luke 19:45-46. Compare these passages from the end of Jesus' ministry to John 2:12-25, which takes place at the beginning of Jesus' ministry. How are they similar? How are they different?

memory verse of the week

Did a particular verse make you think? Is there a verse you can't get out of your head? Write it down and memorize it. Allow God's Word to permanently brand itself in your head and your heart.

notes from group discussion

the Pharisees
sniff out Jesus

Lesson 4

"**The** Father loves the Son and has placed everything in his hands. Whoever believes in the Son has eternal life, but whoever rejects the Son will not see life, for God's wrath remains on him."

John 3:35-36

Put yourself in the place of a Pharisee at the time of Jesus. You're a noble person – noble enough, anyway. You're an expert on the Law of Moses, and you know for a fact that you don't like the Sadducees. They are just wrong, wrong, wrong (think of the modern-day division between Republicans and Democrats).

The Sadducees are livid with Jesus for cleaning out the temple. That's their home turf, and He let them – and everyone else – know they weren't treating it well. But because the Pharisees didn't get along with the Sadducees, they were probably happy with Jesus for denouncing their rivals. So it only makes sense that a Pharisee named Nicodemus would evaluate Jesus, to see if their views on God line up.

Read the third chapter of John.

1   Nicodemus was a member of the Sanhedrin, the governmental body that ruled Jewish matters in Jerusalem and elsewhere. Knowing what you've learned about the Pharisee party, what do you suppose was going through Nicodemus's mind when he approached Jesus (3:1-2)?

2   Read Jesus' words in 3:3. What question did He see in Nicodemus's heart?

Wind . . . Spirit (3:8). The Greek word *pneuma* means "spirit," "breath," and "wind." The breath of a person represents his or her life—when the breath is gone, so is life. Here, the wind of God and the Spirit of God are considered to be like God's breath; it is present in those "born from above"; therefore, they have life.

fyi

3   Explain Jesus' answer to Nicodemus (3:3,5-8) in your own words.

4   Why is new birth, not just right thinking and good living, necessary for seeing and entering God's kingdom?

fyi *Lifted up (3:14).* John is fond of words with double meanings, and here this can mean lifting someone up either in exaltation or physically.[1] Or both.

5   Jesus had barely begun His ministry, but He already seemed to know quite a bit about His mission. Read 3:14-15 and summarize.

fyi • *Loved (3:16).* John uses the word *agape* here, which is a willful, deliberate type of love, not a love based on emotion. God freely chose to love the world.

• *Gave (3:16).* This word has a double meaning: God gave His Son by sending Him into the world and gave Him again on the cross.

6   Read 3:16-18. What does it tell us about God the Father? Jesus the Son?

7   Read 3:19-21. If Jesus came to help the world and put it right again, why do so many people run from Him?

8   In 3:27-30, John the Baptist puts himself below Jesus. What does this tell you about John the Baptist's character?

live

9   Consider John 3:16-17. How does this truth change you? Is there any deeply rooted bitterness or anger that prevents you from accepting this truth? How can you overcome that?

10 Consider the way you act. Does it point toward darkness or God-light? How happy would you be if God's light were to shine on *all* your current practices and habits?

11 How does John the Baptist's attitude toward himself as compared to Jesus give you an example to follow?

connect

In your group, discuss the concept of being "born again." If you didn't know anything about Christianity, what would you think if someone told you that you needed to be born again? Consider 3:16-21 and all the implications it contains. Talk it through, trying to look past the catchphrase-like nature of the passage, and dig into what Jesus is really saying. Finally, pray together and thank God for sending His Son and for giving each of you the ability to choose light.

go deeper

Read 3:13-15. Then, to gain a greater understanding of the serpent, read Numbers 21:4-9. What sort of comparison is Jesus making here?

memory verse of the week

Did a particular verse make you think? Is there a verse you can't get out of your head? Write it down and memorize it. Allow God's Word to permanently brand itself in your head and your heart.

notes from group discussion

opportunity knocks in Samaria

Jesus answered, "Everyone who drinks this water will be thirsty again, but whoever drinks the water I give him will never thirst. Indeed, the water I give him will become in him a spring of water welling up to eternal life."

John 4:13-14

Has a short detour that at first annoyed you ever turned into something that worked out better for you? Have you ever hurried into a store looking for one particular item, only to find a better version of it on sale? Or maybe you've struck up a conversation with someone only to find an unexpected soul connection? Sometimes what seems like a detour or annoyance turns into something quite valuable.

Jesus takes advantage of an unexpected encounter, right in the middle of His ministry, just as He is starting to gain popularity. The Pharisees take notice of Him, but they're beginning to wonder if He's on their side. Jesus knows what they're thinking, but it isn't yet time for Him to deal with them, so He begins to focus His ministry on Galilee. And that is where an unexpected meeting in Samaria becomes a ministry opportunity.

Read the fourth chapter of John.

- *He had to go through Samaria (4:4).* This wasn't for any geographical reason; it had to do with Jesus' mission. The Samaritans practiced a corrupted form of Judaism, where they only regarded the books of Moses as Scripture, and they didn't make sacrifices at Jerusalem. Because of this, the Jews and Samaritans didn't get along, and Samaritans would often refuse to give overnight shelter to Jews who were traveling between Jerusalem and Galilee. Many Jews just avoided Samaria altogether. But not Jesus.

- *I . . . am he (4:26).* This is the only time before His trial that Jesus admits to being the Messiah. He knew that, while the Jews were looking for a mighty political king, the Samaritans were looking only for a prophet and a teacher. They wouldn't get the wrong idea about Him.

- *Talking with a woman (4:27).* In general, rabbis avoided talking with women, even those in their own families.[1] For Jesus to talk to a woman — one He wasn't even related to — would've been unthinkable for the rabbis of His time.

1 Using evidence from Jesus' conversation with the woman at the well, write how He feels about the Samaritans.

2   Who does the woman identify Jesus as in the following verses?

      4:9

      4:11

      4:19

      4:29

3   How does Jesus lead the woman to the conclusion of knowing who He really is?

4 What did the disciples take away from Jesus' encounter with the Samaritan woman (4:31-38)? What did they learn about Jesus? About themselves? About their mission?

5 Check out 4:48. What is wrong with the kind of faith that is sustained by miraculous signs and wonders?

Signs and wonders (4:48). This phrase suggests something **fyi** that is purely spectacular and amazing, which would of course have interested people. Unfortunately, they weren't interested in the other signs Jesus was showing them, signs that pointed to God and that required a response of faith and allegiance.[2]

live

6 Who are the Samaritans in your world – the outcasts with what you see as a flawed worldview? How do you treat them? How should you treat them? How can you lead them to the conclusion of knowing who Jesus really is?

7   When Jesus reveals the woman's immoral life, she tries to change the subject. Do you do this to Him? Think about *why* Jesus exposes your sin, and how He wants you to respond to it.

8   Examine the Samaritan woman's actions *after* she met Jesus. How often do you act like this?

9   What one truth from this chapter stands out to you? Why?

connect

This chapter is full of discussion material, such as how Jesus interacted with the woman at the well or how He went about healing the official's son. What do these events say to your group? Individually, encourage each other by sharing a time when you seized an opportunity for ministry that presented itself. Pray that all members of the group will keep their eyes open for ways to introduce Jesus into situations in their lives.

Write down your answer to question 9. Research this truth in a concordance or other study aid to find out what the rest of the Bible has to say about it.

memory verse of the week

Did a particular verse make you think? Is there a verse you can't get out of your head? Write it down and memorize it. Allow God's Word to permanently brand itself in your head and your heart.

notes from group discussion

opposition begins

"**You** diligently study the Scriptures because you think that by them you possess eternal life. These are the Scriptures that testify about me, yet you refuse to come to me to have life."

John 5:39-40

Imagine, for a moment, that you can't move. You're completely paralyzed. You've been this way for years and years, and you desperately want to walk again. There are rumors of a healing method that happens only once in a while, and while you hope to be able to take advantage of this healing, it never happens for you.

And then this guy Jesus pays you a visit. His popularity is spreading. His message is getting out. And now opposition to Him is increasing. He upset the Sadducees with His actions in the temple; now He's going to even things out by upsetting the Pharisees.

Read the fifth chapter of John.

1 What major themes stick out to you in this chapter?

> • *The law forbids (5:10).* The Law of Moses forbids work on **fyi**
> the Sabbath, so the rabbis came up with some guidelines
> on what could be considered work. In their minds — where the law
> should be applied as widely as possible to avoid breaking *any* pos-
> sible rules — carrying a mat on the Sabbath was work, and therefore
> forbidden.

> • *The Father raises the dead (5:21).* Most ordinary Jews, Sadducees
> aside, strongly believed that God (and only God) could raise the
> dead wherever and whenever He wanted to and that He was plan-
> ning to do just that on the last day of the world.

2 Why did Jesus ask the invalid if he wanted to get well?

3 Why doesn't the disabled man answer Jesus' question directly?

4   Read 5:17-27. In what areas does Jesus claim to be equal with God?

• *My testimony is not valid (5:31).* In other words, if what Jesus says is the only evidence of His relation to the Father, He must be lying.

• *Work (5:36).* When Jesus says "work" or "works," He's usually referring to the Father's work, the work that Jesus is doing on earth. These works include the miraculous signs of transformation, healing, and raising the dead, as well as His teaching—just that He is in the world is part of His work. These signs and wonders aren't miraculous to Jesus; they are part of His nature. He's just doing His job.

5   Jesus rebukes the Pharisees in 5:39-44. What faults does He point out? Identify as many as you can.

live

6   What reasons did the invalid have for lying by the pool for so many years? Put yourself in his position. How would you feel if you were the invalid and someone asked you whether you wanted to get well?

7   Are there areas in your own life where you are like the disabled man? How can Jesus change them?

connect

Consider this question: What would you think and say if Jesus asked you if you wanted to get well? Individually, share how you would react to this question. If you're in the mood for some cheesy fun, play a game of musical chairs, with each chair representing a chance to be healed of a lifelong ailment. Use this as an illustration of how the paralytic kept missing his chance to get into the pool. How does it feel to miss out on a chair? Finally, praise God that you don't have to play a game to experience His power at work in your lives.

go deeper

Jesus says in 5:46 that Moses wrote about Him. Enlist the help of some study aids to research what Moses wrote about Jesus and how those writings are relevant to your life today.

memory verse of the week

Did a particular verse make you think? Is there a verse you can't get out of your head? Write it down and memorize it. Allow God's Word to permanently brand itself in your head and your heart.

notes from group discussion

newness and life

Jesus said to them, "I tell you the truth, it is not Moses who has given you the bread from heaven, but it is my Father who gives you the true bread from heaven. For the bread of God is he who comes down from heaven and gives life to the world."

John 6:32-33

It goes without saying, especially in our culture, that new and improved stuff is always better than the old stuff it improved upon. Medicines work faster. Computers store more information. Video games have better resolution. Newness is a welcome part of life.

We've already seen how Jesus' ways are similar to, but more full than, the old ways of Judaism. His wine is better. His body is a new, better temple. Keeping the Law isn't enough to get Pharisees into heaven.

And then there's the life-giving side of Jesus. Living water replaces well water. The court official's son is revived from near-death. The invalid is healed.

Jesus is both newness and life. And He is confounding to the Jewish leaders.

Read the sixth and seventh chapters of John.

• *The miraculous signs he had performed on the sick (6:2).* John leaves out most of this ministry, which you can read about in the Synoptic Gospels (Matthew, Mark, and Luke).

• *The Passover Feast (6:4).* As this was an annual event, between six months and a full year has passed since chapter 5.

• *Gave thanks (6:11).* Jews didn't bless their food; they blessed God for giving them bread from the earth.

1   The feeding of the five thousand (6:1-15) is the first miraculous act of Jesus that involves the disciples. Why do you think He included them?

2   What does this miracle reveal about Jesus' mission and character?

3 When Jesus walks on water (6:16-21), it is a miracle that only His disciples see. What benefit did they gain from being the sole witnesses to this act?

fyi *True bread (6:32).* Manna was only a bit of foreshadowing; Jesus is the real bread. In Jewish culture, bread symbolized the Law, but Jesus, as the real bread, truly satisfies, unlike the Law.

4 Read 6:27-59. Notice that the people want Jesus to reenact the miracle of manna that God used to feed the Israelites for forty years. Make a list of the things Jesus says about the real bread of God.

5 Chapter 7 begins six months after chapter 6, and now the different groups in Jerusalem are positively buzzing about Jesus. What are they saying (7:1,12)?

- *Without having studied (7:15).* Like the rabbis, Jesus was able to quote entire passages of Scripture from memory and to discuss them intelligently. Unlike the rabbis, He'd never studied under another rabbi. This was absolutely unheard of at the time.[1]

- *My teaching is not my own (7:16).* Rabbis always quoted authorities for their important statements to avoid being discredited. Jesus did the same.

6 Why did Jesus think it was appropriate to heal on the Sabbath (7:21-24)?

7 Read 7:25-27 and 40-43. Why did the Jews judge Jesus based on where He was from? How should they have judged His validity?

- *Glorified (7:39).* The Crucifixion. Jesus' greatest shame was also His greatest glory, and He had to die before we could receive the Holy Spirit.

- *A prophet does not come out of Galilee (7:52).* The Pharisees were obviously upset, because they conveniently forgot that Jonah came from Galilee. More than likely, they just detested Galileans, whom they saw as unsophisticated and spiritually lazy.[2]

live

8 The Jews judged Jesus on outward appearances and His hometown. Do you ever do this to people? How should you judge them instead?

9 Read 7:37-39 and picture yourself as the one coming to Him and drinking. What does that mean to you? In what practical ways can you have rivers of living water spilling out of you?

connect

Take this opportunity with your group to interpret Jesus' actions in 6:1-21, as well as the words He says in 6:25-59, taking special care to focus on the meaning of the true bread. How can each of you respond individually to what Jesus has done and said? What about as a group? Pray and encourage each other to implement these responses in your lives over the next week.

go deeper

Compare John 7:37-39 to Isaiah 55:1-2.

Look through chapters 6 and 7 and make a list of all the misunder-standings about Jesus. What is the truth that was being misunder-stood?

memory verse of the week

Did a particular verse make you think? Is there a verse you can't get out of your head? Write it down and memorize it. Allow God's Word to permanently brand itself in your head and your heart.

notes from group discussion

light, sin, and judgment

Lesson 8

"**I** am the light of the world. Whoever follows me will never walk in darkness, but will have the light of life."

John 8:12

There's no such thing as a "dark bulb." We define illumination by the presence of light, and no one has ever (seriously) said, "Who turned on the dark?" The light by which you're reading this book is showing you the contrast between the darkness of the ink in these letters and the relative lightness of the page. Light reveals all, including the darkness of sin.

As we continue in John, the Feast of Tabernacles is over, but while the crowds are heading home, Jesus sticks around to do some more teaching and to reveal Himself to those who would believe Him.

Jesus is the world's Light, and He is about to say so. Simultaneously, He's addressing the issues of sin and judgment that the Pharisees care about so much.

Read the eighth and ninth chapters of John.

• *Caught in adultery (8:3).* The religion scholars and
Pharisees were bending many rules in this situation. First,
two witnesses had to see the act in order to convict. Second, the
man should have been arrested, but wasn't. Third, the woman's hus-
band wasn't present. Fourth, she didn't need to be brought to the
temple court. Fifth, she had a right to a formal trial and execution.

Because everyone knew Jesus' views on the Law, the leaders
assumed He would not push for execution. Their hope was to trap
Him: If He kept quiet, they would stone her anyway, and He would
be partly responsible. If He spoke out, He could be accused of
teaching against the Law.[1]

• *Write (8:6).* Many people have theories about what Jesus wrote,
but no one knows for sure. Roman judges often wrote out their
decisions and then read them out loud. Jesus may have written
down what He was about to say. Or He may have written something
from the Law, such as Exodus 23:1 ("Do not spread false reports. Do
not help a wicked man by being a malicious witness").[2]

1 What was Jesus' goal for the woman? What did He want for
her?

2   What does Jesus claim about Himself in the following verses?

8:12

8:19

8:23

8:29

8:31-32

8:51

8:56-58

9:39

3   What do you think Jesus means when He calls Himself the world's Light?

We . . . have never been slaves (8:33). They're overlooking the Roman rule under which they're currently living.   **fyi**

4   What does the former blind man call Jesus in the following verses, and what do these instances mean?

9:11

9:17

9:33

9:35-38

5   How do these comments add to Jesus' case of being the world's Light?

6   Is suffering ever the result of someone's sin?

The blind will see (9:39). The prophet Isaiah said that the Messiah would restore sight to the blind (Isaiah 29:18; 35:5). Jesus did this kind of miracle more than any other kind.

7   Put yourself in the place of the woman caught in adultery. How would you feel in the midst of this scene? What impressions about Himself would Jesus leave with you?

8   Now put yourself in the place of the accusers and ask yourself the same questions.

9   Read about the blind man's testimony in chapter 9. How are his actions in the face of hostility a model for you?

10   Are you ever like the Pharisees? Do you ever put your preconceived notions of God or Jesus in front of clear evidence that challenges those notions? Pray about this.

74

connect

Turn off the lights and try to make it as dark as possible in the room. Let this soak in for a bit. As a group, while it's still dark, discuss what light symbolizes or represents to each of you. Compare the darkened room to the darkness of a life of sin. Then turn on the lights and draw comparisons between actual light and the world's Light, Jesus. Pray together that you will each be bringers of Christ's light into the darkness of the world around you.

go deeper

See what the other gospels have to say about Jesus as the Light of the World. Then check the rest of the New Testament. Finally, search out the word *light* in the Old Testament. Are there any verses or passages you find that point toward Jesus as the Light?

memory verse of the week

Did a particular verse make you think? Is there a verse you can't get out of your head? Write it down and memorize it. Allow God's Word to permanently brand itself in your head and your heart.

notes from group discussion

rejection and resurrection

"**The** reason my Father loves me is that I lay down my life – only to take it up again. No one takes it from me, but I lay it down of my own accord. I have authority to lay it down and authority to take it up again. This command I received from my Father."

John 10:17-18

Has your mouth ever gotten you in trouble? Even if you spoke the truth, people just didn't want to hear it. No matter how right you were, no matter how tenderly you broached the subject, no matter how much of an expert you were, you just weren't accepted. In fact, you might've been flat-out rejected.

The same thing has happened with Jesus. He's done nothing but speak the truth the whole time He's been ministering. He's been trying to connect with people, and even though the Pharisees and many Jews have rejected Him, He still tries to give them a clue as to who He is. Then, a couple of months later, He restates His identity to them and heads off to the city where John the Baptist started his ministry, knowing that the next time He comes to Jerusalem, He'll be marked for death. Finally, He winds up in Bethany after an important message about a friend.

Read the tenth and eleventh chapters of John.

study

fyi

• *Gate (10:1-3).* In small sheep pens, the shepherd would often become the gate, sleeping in front of the opening to prevent the sheep from wandering and wolves from coming in.

• *Shepherd (10:2,11).* In the Old Testament, God is often described as a shepherd, and because the patriarchs, Moses, and David were all shepherds, the term came to mean "the rulers of God's people." When Israel turned from God, He declared that He would rescue them from wicked shepherds and shepherd them Himself.

• *Voice (10:3-5,16).* Palestinian shepherds had names for each of their sheep, and when two flocks spent the night together, the shepherds sorted out individual sheep by calling their name. The sheep actually do know their name, and the voice of their shepherd.[1]

1   Read 10:1-11. What are the characteristics of the true, Good Shepherd? What do these tell you about Jesus?

2   How are we to recognize thieves and robbers? What would this look like in a modern setting?

3   Jesus calls Himself both the gate and the Good Shepherd. What do these names say about Him?

4   Read 10:35-38. What is Jesus' point in saying this? What is His evidence that His claims are true?

5   In the story of Lazarus (11:1-44), why did Jesus stay where He was for two days after receiving word that Lazarus was ill?

6   Why does John stress Jesus' love for Mary, Martha, and Lazarus?

7   The raising of Lazarus is the last miracle mentioned in John that Jesus performs before His own resurrection. What does it reveal about His character? His mission?

8   Read the reaction of the Jewish leaders to this miracle in 11:45-48. What was wrong with their reaction?

The Romans will come (11:48). The Romans didn't tolerate disorder, so they were always ready to stamp out any potential revolts.

fyi

live

9   What happens when you, as a sheep, know and follow the Good Shepherd? What is involved in that kind of relationship?

10 What implications does Lazarus's resuscitation have for you personally?

connect

As a group, consider Jesus' reaction to the death of Lazarus, compared to the crowd's. Think of a time when you lost a loved one and share it with the group if you'd like. How did you feel about yourself? About God? Pray together to gain God's perspective on death, and pray that you'll be able to lean on each other when face-to-face with mortality.

go deeper

Study up on the Old Testament patriarchs. Which ones were shepherds? What were their stories? How do those stories relate to Jesus as the Good Shepherd?

memory verse of the week

Did a particular verse make you think? Is there a verse you can't get out of your head? Write it down and memorize it. Allow God's Word to permanently brand itself in your head and your heart.

notes from group discussion

back to Jerusalem

"**The** hour has come for the Son of Man to be glorified. I tell you the truth, unless a kernel of wheat falls to the ground and dies, it remains only a single seed. But if it dies, it produces many seeds."

John 12:23-24

Okay, think about the most newsworthy thing you've heard in the past year. Got it? Now, imagine that you heard about it only by word of mouth and even *that* bit of information was whispered in your ear because the government, the police, and everyone else in charge have banned such discussion.

The news about Lazarus's resurrection has reached Jerusalem, and people are stirring, quietly. Could this man Jesus be the Messiah? No one's officially allowed to talk about it (even though they are talking about it), because the Jewish ruling body has decreed that Jesus is a criminal, and harboring Him in any way is a punishable offense. Meanwhile, Jesus has laid low since the miracle, and now people are wondering if He'll defy the Jewish rulers and show up in Jerusalem for Passover.

The people, however, couldn't predict what Jesus would do when He did show up. Neither could His disciples, who didn't know that dinner would take an unexpected turn.

Read the twelfth and thirteenth chapters of John.

study

• *A pint of pure nard, an expensive perfume (12:3).*
fyi
It was customary for oil like this to be poured over the
head of a guest of honor. To pour it on Jesus' feet, however, was
extremely humble. Further, a woman's hair was her glory, and for
Mary to use it to wipe the lowly feet was about as devoted as it got.

• *A year's wages (12:5).* Judas Iscariot would later betray Jesus for a
tenth of this annual salary, a mere thirty silver pieces (see Matthew
26:14-16).

1 Why did Mary do what she did in 12:3?

• *The chief priests (12:9-11).* As if plotting Jesus' death
fyi
wasn't enough, now they're talking of killing Lazarus too.
The Sadducees didn't believe in resurrection, so to them, Lazarus
was a walking impossibility, but instead of changing their beliefs,
they resort to murder.

• *The great crowd (12:12).* More than likely, these were people
who'd come to Jerusalem from Galilee to celebrate the feast. Many
of them had no doubt seen Jesus' miracles in person, and when
they heard He was coming to the feast, they went to meet Him.
They'd already tried once to call Him Messiah, which He resisted
(6:14-15), but this time He received their praise and they loved it.

88

- *Young donkey (12:14-15).* Again Jesus asserts the true meaning of the Messiah. If He were to be a conquering king, He would've ridden in on a warhorse. But a king on a peaceful mission would ride an unbroken donkey.

2 Why did Jesus accept the public acclaim this time, when He'd rejected it earlier?

3 Consider this scene carefully. Why is it important? Why did John include it in his gospel?

4 Read 12:20-23. Why did the coming of the Greeks signal to Jesus that it was time for Him to be glorified?

5 Why would Jesus use a word like *glorified*? How is the humiliation and shame of the Cross "glorification"?

fyi   *Wash his disciples' feet (13:5).* A menial task. Guests' feet were usually washed as soon as they came into the home, but Jesus did it in the middle of dinner in order to prove a point.

6   Read 13:1-5. How would you describe Jesus' attitude?

7   Why does Peter object in 13:6-8?

8   How does Jesus counter this objection?

9   Read 13:18-30. Why did Jesus predict Judas's deceit in such a nonspecific way? Why didn't He just call Judas out for the traitor that he was?

10   Continue on and read 13:31-38. Jesus has Judas out of the way and begins to say a few last things to His true disciples. What is the "new command" that He gives them in 13:34-35?

11 How is this command ironic, knowing what Judas and Peter are about to do?

12 How does the foot-washing help explain this command?

live

13 Read 12:24-26. How is this relevant to you? How can you be "reckless in your love" (verse 25, MSG)?

14 Reflect on 13:1-17. Whose feet do you figuratively need to wash? How can you do that? Remember that Jesus also received a foot-washing earlier; who is washing *your* feet? How can you thank them?

15 Read 13:36-38. Peter had a hotheaded devotion to Jesus. How would you describe your devotion?

connect

What is the most menial or unpleasant act of service that some-one has done for you lately? What about something you've done for someone else? If your group wants to, consider conducting an actual foot-washing ceremony, symbolically representing your group's com-mitment to support each other, even in the uncomfortable places in life. Pray for a stronger bond among your group's members, and praise Jesus for washing you so completely in His humility and love.

go deeper

Study Zechariah 9:9-13 to gain some context of Jesus' entry into Jerusalem. Also, consult Zephaniah 3:14-17 to compare.

memory verse of the week

Did a particular verse make you think? Is there a verse you can't get out of your head? Write it down and memorize it. Allow God's Word to permanently brand itself in your head and your heart.

notes from group discussion

last words

"**Do** not let your hearts be troubled. Trust in God; trust also in me. In my Father's house are many rooms; if it were not so, I would have told you. I am going there to prepare a place for you."

John 14:1-2

Have you ever given more than a passing thought to what your last words will be? Not your official last words, the ones you whisper seconds before you die, but what you would say to those you love if you knew you were dying. What wisdom would you want to impart to them? What do you *really* want them to know about you?

For Jesus, it's getting close to that time. In less than twenty-four hours He will die. It'll probably be less than six before He gets arrested. Jesus is sitting with His eleven closest friends, the men who will carry on His name and work, those who will establish the church. He's in anguish, but He knows He must prepare these men for the work they will inherit.

And then, just before He gives up His freedom, He seeks His heavenly Father and prays in earnest for the disciples He loves.

Read chapters 14 through 17 of John. (This is a long reading, to be sure, but it'll be worth it in the end, I promise.)

study

1   What is the main point John wants to get across in each of these chapters?

2   Examine 14:1–16:33. What does Jesus say about the Father?

The Son?

The Holy Spirit?

Prayer?

96

Peace?

Love?

Obedience?

3   The disciples are grief-stricken to learn that their master will be leaving them. But what will they gain, according to the following verses?

14:2-3

14:12

14:13-14

4   What does Jesus mean when He says He is "the way" (14:6)? What about "the truth"? "The life"?

- *In my name (14:13-14,26; 15:16; 16:23-24,26).* Jesus' name is not the key variable in a prayer request formula. He isn't teaching algebra. Instead, He's talking about praying along the same lines and with the same character as His name. Your prayers should line up with His teaching and all He stands for.

- *Peace (14:27).* This word, *shalom,* is a standard greeting and farewell in Hebrew, but that's not how Jesus used it. It is not a mere wish, but a real, effective peace. It is not the absence of war, so to speak, but vitality and wholeness in every part of life.

5   Read 14:22-24. Write in your own words Jesus' reasons for not showing Himself to the world.

6   How is it possible to be joined with Jesus (15:1-9)?

7   Read 15:18–16:4. Why should Christians expect to be persecuted? Why did Jesus warn His disciples – and us – about this?

fyi **Sin and righteousness and judgment (16:8).** The world didn't understand these three things, and so they decided that Jesus was a sinner, that the Jewish leaders and the Roman rulers were righteous, and therefore that Jesus deserved to be judged and executed.

8   According to chapter 17, what has the Father given the Son? What has the Son given to His disciples?

fyi **Sanctify (17:17-19).** To make holy. To separate from the world's outlook and control. To be committed to the outlook and guidance of the Holy Spirit.

9 Why is unity among believers, the Father, and the Son so critical (17:21,23)?

10 Chapters 14, 15, and 16 are some of Jesus' most profound teachings. Using your answers to question 2, how can you implement the Lord's teachings on these subjects in your own life?

11 How can you love other Christians as Jesus loved His disciples? As He has loved you? Think of five practical ways.

12 Jesus said His followers would do greater things than He did (14:12). Does this apply to you? If so, are you doing what Jesus said you would/should do? Pray about this.

connect

Start by reading 15:17-18 aloud. Talk these verses through as a group, maybe putting them into your own words. Share a time when you've experienced hostility or scorn because of your faith. What did you do? What should you have done? Encourage each other in your faith, and pray for wisdom when you encounter hostility for your beliefs, that you'll be able to react to it in the same way Jesus did.

go deeper

Read John 15:1-8, then compare it to 1 Corinthians 12:12-26. What do Jesus' images of the vine and Paul's images of the body of Christ have in common? What do these passages tell you about your relationships, both with Jesus and with other Christians?

memory verse of the week

Did a particular verse make you think? Is there a verse you can't get out of your head? Write it down and memorize it. Allow God's Word to permanently brand itself in your head and your heart.

notes from group discussion

arrest, trial, torture, execution

Lesson 12

When he had received the drink, Jesus said, "It is finished." With that, he bowed his head and gave up his spirit.

John 19:30

It's like the plot of just about every Hollywood police potboiler: Arrested for a Crime He Didn't Commit. But in those movies, the protagonist always manages to elude the authorities long enough to clear his name, and by the end, he's free and loving it.

Of course, it doesn't happen quite that way for Jesus. After His prayer, Jesus and His disciples head to an olive grove on the slopes of the Mount of Olives called Gethsemane. John skips over Jesus' anguished prayer to His father (found in Luke 22:40-46), taking us instead to the moment of betrayal. Then comes the arrest, the trial, the torture, and the execution.

Ask God to impress Jesus' character on your heart as you read the eighteenth and nineteenth chapters of John.

1 Review 18:1-11. Dig deeply by answering these questions:

Who was there?

What was going on?

When did it happen?

Where did it happen?

Why did it happen?

How did it happen?

fyi • *A detachment of soldiers and some officials from the chief priests and Pharisees (18:3).* The Jewish ruling body sent part of the temple guard; the Roman governor sent part of his army. Both governments assumed Jesus was a dangerous rebel who was hiding out and did not expect Him to go without a fight.[1]

• *Sword (18:10).* The original language here denotes a long dagger, or a short sword. Carrying weapons during feast times was illegal,[2] but Peter must've known something was up to break the law like he did.

2 Think about what's happening to Jesus here, and how He responds to it. What does this tell you about Him?

fyi *Questioned (18:19).* Jewish legal procedure indicated that people were innocent unless two witnesses gave agreeing testimony and that the accused could not be asked to incriminate themselves. This interrogation was unofficial, as Annas was trying to figure out whether Jesus had been training His disciples to start an uprising, but Jesus, knowing the customs, made sure Annas stuck to the law.[3]

3 What attitudes does Jesus show toward Himself and others in 18:19-23?

4 Take a look at Luke 6:27-31. How is John 18:22-23 consistent with this passage?

5 What do you learn about Peter's character in this week's reading?

- *Early morning (18:28).* Jewish law stated that death sentences could not be handed out at night, which is why this trial started so early. Also, Roman courts generally began at daybreak, so the timing of Jesus' interview with Pilate is not unusual.[4]

- *Pilate (18:29).* Pontius Pilate was prefect of Judah from AD 26 to 36, and the Jews hated him. On one occasion, a Jewish holy day, he had his soldiers parade down the street, carrying a portrait of the emperor, which the Jews saw as an idol. Enraged by this blasphemy, the Jews rioted, gaining Pilate a severe reprimand from his superiors. When presented with Jesus, Pilate wanted to prevent another riot over a Messiah in order to avoid more punishment from Rome.[5]

- *No right to execute (18:31).* Romans preferred the Jews to govern other Jews by their own laws, but one thing the Romans wouldn't allow was a death sentence. Additionally, the Jewish ruling body would prefer that Jesus be crucified instead of stoned, as stoning would make Jesus look like a martyred prophet. Death by crucifixion was more dishonorable, and proof of God's rejection.[6]

6   Why was it necessary for Jesus to die on a cross? See Galatians 3:13 for more information.

7   Of what crimes was Jesus accused (18:30,33; 19:7,19)?

8   What evidence was there for or against these accusations?

9   Jesus refuses to answer Pilate's question in 19:9. Why? Why did He answer the rest of them?

10   What do Pilate's words and actions tell you about him?

- *Crucified (19:18).* This was a horrible, painful means of death, usually taking hours before the victim's heart failed from the combination of blood loss from the scourging, the heat of the unrelenting sun, and restricted circulation and breathing. Only the lowest of the low—criminals and slaves—were crucified, as it was an unspeakable disgrace to die in this manner.[7]

fyi

- *It is finished (19:30).* In Greek, this phrase is one word, *tetelestai,* a word that has shown up on ancient invoices found in Egypt. It is highly possible that this word was written on the invoice once a debt had been paid in full.

11 Looking over John's crucifixion narrative, we can see that he left out many things that appear in the Synoptic Gospels (Matthew, Mark, and Luke). So the things he left *in* must be things he considered important. With John in mind, what's the importance of Pilate's wording of Jesus' charge?

The soldiers casting lots for Jesus' clothes?

Jesus giving His mother into John's care?

Jesus' thirst?

Jesus' legs remaining unbroken? His side being stabbed with a spear?

12 Read 19:38-42. As Jewish officials who were secret disciples of Jesus, what were Joseph and Nicodemus risking by asking for Jesus' body and burying it?

13 Is there significance to this, considering that all of Jesus' other disciples had fled?

live

14 What parts of Jesus' trial and execution mean the most to you personally? Why?

15 What do Jesus' words "It is finished" mean to you?

connect

Secure a piece of wood (a small plank will do), a few short nails, a hammer, and some index cards. As a means of connecting with each other and with the sacrifice Jesus made for each of you, discuss the Crucifixion and the personal implications it has. Reflect on your personal sins that Jesus died for and think of a particular sin or vice that you're struggling with at the moment. Remember – none of us is perfect, and we all have things about ourselves that Jesus needs to change. Write that down on an index card, then individually attach the card to the wood by driving a nail through it. As the nails pierce the cards, remember it as a symbol of Jesus' flesh being pierced. Leave your "sins" on the wood. Pray as a group that you'll each have the strength to "nail your sins to the cross." (Note: A corkboard and pushpins can be substituted for the wood and nails.)

go deeper

None of the four Gospels gives a full account of every trial Jesus endured. Make a list of the Jewish and Roman trials that appear in all four Gospels, then study them to get a complete picture of what Jesus endured.

memory verse of the week

Did a particular verse make you think? Is there a verse you can't get out of your head? Write it down and memorize it. Allow God's Word to permanently brand itself in your head and your heart.

notes from group discussion

life and beyond

Again Jesus said, "Peace be with you! As the Father has sent me, I am sending you." And with that he breathed on them and said, "Receive the Holy Spirit."

John 20:21-22

In the polar regions, the oceans are covered by ice. Sheets of it float on the surface, forming a thick cap over the water. Find your way into the ocean, and you'll have a very difficult time finding your way out; the ice caps are too heavy to lift or dig through, and the cold water will be too much of a shock to your system anyway.

This is an approximation of how the disciples feel. After all, it is done. Jesus is dead, and by the end of the day, He is buried. His disciples go into hiding, nursing their broken dreams, numb with grief, drowning slowly in the icy water of depression. And then something startling happens, and continues for forty days afterward.

Read the twentieth and twenty-first chapters of John.

• **Stone had been removed (20:1).** The original Greek here implies not that the stone had simply been rolled away, but that it had been violently removed.[1]

• **Folded up (20:7).** In contrast with the violence of the stone's removal, here John describes order. Had Jesus' body been stolen, the stone would have been moved just enough to allow passage, and the linens would have been either taken or torn off and scattered.[2]

1   As you look through this week's reading, what evidence do you see of Jesus' resurrection?

2   Look at the following passages. What do they indicate about how Jesus looked after His resurrection?

    20:14; 21:4

    20:19,26

    20:20,27

3   Imagine that you, like Mary Magdalene, were the first person to discover the empty tomb. How would you feel as you stood there? What about when Jesus said your name?

4   Why did Mary not recognize Jesus until after He said her name?

fyi   ***Do not hold on to me (20:17).*** Jesus said this for two reasons. One, He was assuring Mary that He was going to be around for a while, so she didn't need to fear that He would leave. Two, things had very much changed since the Resurrection, but Mary was treating Jesus the same way, as if nothing had changed. She needed to let go of her former concept of Jesus and see Him as He really was: the resurrected Messiah.

5   Is there any significance to the way Jesus talks about God in 20:17?

6   What can we learn from Thomas and the way Jesus treats him (20:24-29)?

7   Why did John include Jesus' appearance to the disciples at the
seashore (21:1-23)?

8   Why did Jesus question Peter's love three times, in front of the
other disciples? Why was love such an essential part of the equation?

live

9   Meditate on the authority Jesus gives the disciples in 20:23.
What is He authorizing them to do? How does this relate to you?

10   Put yourself in Peter's place and think back on the way you've
lived this week. Now, imagine Jesus examining your life and saying,
"Do you love me?" How would your life answer that question?

connect

Discuss the symbolic nailing of your sins to the "cross" that you did last week. Have you seen any changes in your life since then? Take as much time as you need to discuss this. If you have more time, move on to review the gospel of John together. If anyone has any questions about the gospel, try to answer them as a group (if you can, take another week to do this review if your time today is running too short). If you've seen growth in each other, point it out as a form of encouragement. Pray together about what you will do next as a group, and pray that you'll be able to carry on with the things you've each implemented as a result of your study together.

go deeper

Take a broad look at the entire book of John. What did Jesus reveal about Himself in each of His miraculous acts? What was Jesus' mission? What areas of this gospel speak particularly to you?

memory verse of the week

Did a particular verse make you think? Is there a verse you can't get out of your head? Write it down and memorize it. Allow God's Word to permanently brand itself in your head and your heart.

notes from group discussion

study resources

It's true that studying the Bible can often lead you to answers for life's tough questions. But Bible study also prompts plenty of *new* questions. Perhaps you're intrigued by a passage and want to understand it better. Maybe you're stumped about what a particular verse or word means. Where do you go from here? Study resources can help. Research a verse's history, cultural context, and connotations. Look up unfamiliar words. Track down related Scripture passages elsewhere in the Bible. Study resources can help sharpen your knowledge of God's Word.

Below you'll find a selected bibliography of study resources. Use them to discover more, dig deeper, and ultimately grow closer to God.

a study resource collection

TH1NK REFERENCE COLLECTION: *The Bible: Think for Yourself About What's Inside; Theology: Think for Yourself About What You Believe; Worldviews: Think for Yourself About How We See God.* Colorado Springs, CO: NavPress, 2006.

historical and background sources

Carson, D. A., Douglas Moo, and Leon Morris. *An Introduction to the New Testament.* Grand Rapids, MI: Zondervan, 1992.
> *Provides an overview of the New Testament for students and teachers. Covers historical and biographical information and includes outlines and discussions of each book's theological importance.*

Packer, James I., Merrill C. Tenney, and William White Jr. *The Bible Almanac.* Nashville: Nelson, 1980.

Contains information about people of the Bible and how they lived. Photos and illustrations help the characters come to life.

Tenney, Merrill C. *New Testament Survey.* Grand Rapids, MI: Eerdmans, 1985.
Analyzes social, political, cultural, economic, and religious backgrounds of each New Testament book.

concordances, dictionaries, and atlases

Concordances

If you are studying a specific word and want to know where to find it in the Bible, use a concordance. A concordance lists every verse in the Bible in which that word shows up. An *exhaustive* concordance includes every word in a given translation (there are different concordances for different Bible translations), and an *abridged* or *complete* concordance leaves out some words, some occurrences of the words, or both. Multiple varieties exist, so choose for yourself which one you like best. *Strong's Exhaustive Concordance* and *Young's Analytical Concordance of the Bible* are the most popular.

Bible Dictionaries

Sometimes called a *Bible encyclopedia*, a Bible dictionary alphabetically lists articles about people, places, doctrines, important words, customs, and geography of the Bible. Here are a few to consider:

The New Strong's Expanded Dictionary of Bible Words. Nashville: Nelson, 2001.
Defines more than 14,000 words. In addition, it includes an index that gives meanings of the word in the original language.

Nelson's New Illustrated Bible Dictionary. Nashville: Nelson, 1996.
Includes over 500 photos, maps, and pronunciation guides.

The New Unger's Bible Dictionary. Wheaton, IL: Moody, 1988.
>   *Displays pictures, maps, and illustrations. Clearly written, easy to understand, and compatible with most Bible translations.*

Vine's Expository Dictionary of New Testament Words. Peabody, MA: Hendrickson, 1993.
>   *Lists major words and defines each New Testament Greek word.*

Bible Atlases

We often skim over mentions of specific locations in the Bible, but location is an important element to understanding the context of a passage. A Bible atlas can help you understand the geography in a book of the Bible and how it may have affected the recorded events. Here are two good choices:

The Illustrated Bible Atlas. Grand Rapids, MI: Kregel, 1999.
>   *Provides concise (and colorful) information on lands and cities where events took place. Includes historical notes.*

The Carta Bible Atlas. Jerusalem: Carta, 2003.
>   *Includes analytical notes on biblical events, military campaigns, travel routes, and archeological highlights, as well as indexes. A very popular atlas for students, scholars, and clergy.*

for small-group leaders

If you are the leader of a small group or would like to lead a small group, these resources may help:

Beyerlein, Ann. *Small Group Leaders' Handbook.* Downers Grove, IL: InterVarsity, 1995.
>   *Teaches the biblical basis and growth stages of small groups. Helps leaders develop skills for resolving conflict, leading discussion, and planning for the future.*

McBride, Neal F. *How to Lead Small Groups.* Colorado Springs, CO: NavPress, 1990.

Covers leadership skills for all kinds of small groups. Filled with step-by-step guidance and practical exercises focusing on the most important aspects of small-group leadership.

Polich, Laurie. *Help! I'm a Small-Group Leader.* Grand Rapids, MI: Zondervan, 1998.

Offers tips and solutions to help you nurture your small group and accomplish your goals. Suggests techniques and questions to use in many Bible study circumstances.

bible study methods

Fee, Gordon, and Douglas Stuart. *How to Read the Bible for All Its Worth.* Grand Rapids, MI: Zondervan, 2003.

Offers chapters on interpreting and applying the different kinds of writing in the Bible: the Epistles, the Gospels, Old Testament Law, Old Testament narrative, the Prophets, Psalms, Wisdom Literature, and Revelation. Also includes suggestions for commentaries on each book of the Bible.

LaHaye, Tim. *How to Study the Bible for Yourself.* Eugene, OR: Harvest House, 1998.

Teaches how to illuminate Scripture through study. Gives methods for understanding the Bible's major principles, promises, commands, key verses, and themes.

Wald, Oletta. *The New Joy of Discovery in Bible Study.* Minneapolis: Augsburg, 2002.

Helps students of Scripture discover how to observe all that is in a text, how to ask questions of a text, and how to use grammar and passage structure to see the writer's point. Teaches methods for independent Bible study.

notes

Introduction to John: The Beloved Story

1. Few scholars today, besides conservative evangelicals, believe the ancient tradition that the apostle John wrote this gospel. But the unanimous opinion of the church from AD 180 onward (we have no clear records before then) is that the author was John the apostle. If you want to research this on your own, consult commentaries. For starters, try *The Gospel According to John* by Raymond E. Brown and *Studies in the Fourth Gospel* by Leon Morris.

Lesson 3: The Beginning of Miracles

1. Leon Morris, *The Gospel According to John* (Grand Rapids, MI: Eerdmaus, 1971), 178; Raymond E. Brown, *The Gospel According to John (I–XII), The Anchor Bible*, vol. 29 (New York: Doubleday, 1966), 97.
2. Morris, 177.
3. F. F. Bruce, *New Testament History* (New York: Doubleday, 1971), 189–190.

Lesson 4: The Pharisees Sniff Out Jesus

1. Leon Morris, *The Gospel According to John* (Grand Rapids, MI: Eerdmans, 1971), 225–226.

Lesson 5: Opportunity Knocks in Samaria

1. Leon Morris, *The Gospel According to John* (Grand Rapids, MI: Eerdmans, 1971), 274.
2. Morris, 290.

Lesson 7: Newness and Life

1. Leon Morris, *The Gospel According to John* (Grand Rapids, MI: Eerdmans, 1971), 404–405.
2. Morris, 434, note 108.

Lesson 8: Light, Sin, and Judgment

1. Leon Morris, *The Gospel According to John* (Grand Rapids, MI: Eerdmans, 1971), 885.
2. Morris, 886–888; compare Raymond E. Brown, *The Gospel According to John (I–XII), The Anchor Bible*, vol. 29 (New York: Doubleday, 1966), 337.

Lesson 9: Rejection and Resurrection

1. Leon Morris, *The Gospel According to John* (Grand Rapids, MI: Eerdmans, 1971), 502, note 17; Raymond E. Brown, *The Gospel According to John (I–XII), The Anchor Bible*, vol. 29 (New York: Doubleday, 1966), 385.
2. Morris, 546.

Lesson 12: Arrest, Trial, Torture, Execution

1. F. F. Bruce, *New Testament History* (Garden City, NY: Doubleday, 1980), 195–196.
2. Leon Morris, *The Gospel According to John* (Grand Rapids, MI: Eerdmans, 1971), 745, note 15.
3. William Barclay, *The Gospel of John*, vol. 2 (Philadelphia: Westminster, 1956), 61.
4. Morris, 752.
5. J. I. Packer, Merrill C. Tenney, and William White Jr., *The World of the New Testament* (Nashville: Nelson, 1972), 82.
6. Morris, 765-766.
7. E. Brandenburger, "Cross," *New International Dictionary of New Testament Theology*, vol. 1 (Grand Rapids, MI: Zondervan, 1975), 391–393.

Lesson 13: Life and Beyond

1. Leon Morris, *The Gospel According to John* (Grand Rapids, MI: Eerdmans, 1971), 831.
2. Morris, 833.
3. Morris, 855, note 80.

MORE DOUBLE-EDGED BIBLE STUDIES FROM THINK BOOKS.

 ### THINK:LIFECHANGE Mark
The Navigators
978-1-57683-692-7
This close look at the first of the written Gospels will help you encounter God in a new way.

 ### THINK:LIFECHANGE James
The Navigators
978-1-57683-691-0
This in-depth study of James will empower you to grow spiritually and go deeper into God's Word.

 ### THINK:LIFECHANGE Ruth & Esther
The Navigators
978-1-57683-852-5
Young women will find two strong examples of women who lived for God, no matter what the cost.

 ### THINK:LIFECHANGE Romans
The Navigators
978-1-57683-850-1
With this fresh study of Romans, you'll learn to identify, study, and apply foundational theological concepts.

 ### THINK:LIFECHANGE Ephesians
The Navigators
978-1-60006-000-7
Study the history, context, and themes of Ephesians. Learn how Paul's advice can help you turn belief into behavior.

To order copies, visit your local Christian bookstore,
call NavPress at 1-800-366-7788, or log on to www.navpress.com.
To locate a Christian bookstore near you, call 1-800-991-7747.